AN ANALYSIS OF
THE PRODUCT-SPECIFIC RULES
OF ORIGIN OF THE REGIONAL
COMPREHENSIVE ECONOMIC
PARTNERSHIP

APRIL 2022

ᴬIAN DEVELOPMENT BANK

Creative Commons Attribution 3.0 IGO license (CC BY 3.0 IGO)

Notes:
In this publication, "$" refers to United States dollars.
ADB recognizes "Korea" as the Republic of Korea.

On the cover: The Regional Comprehensive Economic Partnership (RCEP) has significant potential in facilitating trade
across Asia and the Pacific (photo by Ariel Javellana/ADB).

Cover design by Francis Joseph Manio.

Contents

Tables and Figures   iv

Acknowledgments   v

Abbreviations   vi

Executive Summary   vii

Introduction   viii

I.   Main Features of RCEP Rules of Origin   1
II.   The Form of PSRO in RCEP, ATIGA, and CPTPP   4
III. Methodology to Assess PSRO Stringency or Leniency in RCEP   11
IV.   Codifying PSRO Stringency and Leniency in RCEP   17
V.   Matching the Results of Coding with Trade and Tariff Data   25
VI.   Conclusions and Recommendations   31

References   33

Tables and Figures

Tables

1	Comparison of Definition of Originating Products	2
2	Comparison of RVC Calculations	3
3	Example of Different Uses of CTC and Drafting Techniques	5
4	Summary of PSRO	6
5	Classification of PSRO	7
6	Assessing PSRO Using Manufacturing Requirements	12
7	Meat Products	13
8	Flours	13
9	Article of Plastics	14
10	Clothing of Chapter 62	15
11	Footwear	15
12	Monitors	16
13	Results of the PSRO Coding	19
14	Results of PSRO Coding with the Exclusion of HS Chapters 50–63	20
15	Simple Coding	21
16	Simple Coding Excluding HS Chapters 50–63	22
17	Convergence Count Summary	23
18	Full Convergence	23
19	Partial Convergence I	24
20	Partial Convergence II	24
21	RCEP Intra-Imports, 2019	26
22	MFN rates and RCEP Intra-Imports, 2019	29

Figures

1	RCEP, ATIGA, and CPTPP Membership	ix
2	ATIGA Product-Specific Rules of Origin	8
3	RCEP Product-Specific Rules of Origin	9
4	CPTPP Product-Specific Rules of Origin	10
5	Distribution of Intra-RCEP Trade, 2019	21

Acknowledgments

This report was prepared by the Regional Cooperation and Integration Division (ERCI) of the Economic Research and Regional Cooperation Department (ERCD) of the Asian Development Bank (ADB). It was supported by the ADB technical assistance project, Raising the Value of Regional Trade Agreements—Key Factors for Successful Implementation and Positive Economic Impact (TA 6740), financed by ADB's Technical Assistance Special Fund and the Regional Cooperation and Integration Fund. The authors are Pramila Crivelli, ERCI economist; Stefano Inama, chief at the United Nations Conference on Trade and Development (UNCTAD); and Mark Pearson, ADB consultant. Paulo Rodelio Halili and Pramila Crivelli coordinated the production of this report under the supervision of Cyn-Young Park, director, ERCI.

James Unwin edited the manuscript, Francis Joseph Manio created the cover design, and Michael Cortes implemented the typesetting and layout. Jess Macasaet proofread the report, while Ma. Cecilia Abellar handled the page proof checking, with support from Paulo Rodelio Halili. The Printing Services Unit of ADB's Corporate Services Department and the Publishing Team of the Department of Communications supported printing and publishing.

Abbreviations

ADB	Asian Development Bank
ASEAN	Association of Southeast Asian Nations
ATIGA	ASEAN Trade in Goods Agreement
CC	Change of Chapter
CPTPP	Comprehensive and Progressive Agreement for Trans-Pacific Partnership
CR	Chemical Reaction rule
CTC	Change of Tariff Classification
CTH	Change of Tariff Heading
CTSH	Change of Tariff Sub-Heading
ERCI	Regional Cooperation and Integration Division
EU	European Union
GSP	Generalized System of Preferences
FOB	Freight on Board
FTA	Free Trade Agreement
FVNM	Focused Value of Non-Originating Materials
HS	Harmonized System
MFN	Most-Favored Nation
NC	Net Cost
PRC	People's Republic of China
PSRO	Product-Specific Rules of Origin
RCEP	Regional Comprehensive Economic Partnership
RoO	Rules of Origin
RVC	Regional Value Content
UNCTAD	United Nations Conference on Trade and Development
VNM	Value of Non-Originating Materials
VOM	Value of Originating Materials
WO	Wholly Obtained

Executive Summary

There are more than 30 free trade agreements (FTAs) applying different rules of origin across Asia and the Pacific. And the number continues to grow. One of the perceived advantages of the Regional Comprehensive Economic Partnership (RCEP) is its potential for unifying the "noodle bowl" of diverse rules of origin in the region through its wide membership, cumulation provisions, and the establishment of a common set of rules among member economies. RCEP includes the 10 members of the Association of Southeast Asian Nations (ASEAN), the People's Republic of China (PRC), Japan, the Republic of Korea, along with Australia and New Zealand.

This study examines whether RCEP can concretely seize this unifying opportunity. Such an outcome depends on how RCEP deals with the following determinants:

    (i) ensuring a competitive preferential margin by way of deeper tariff cuts compared to existing FTAs;

    (ii) providing clear and predictable provisions allowing effective and business-friendly cumulation of originating inputs and of working and processing operations carried out in the RCEP region, including tariff differentials;

    (iii) easing product-specific rules of origin (PSRO) compared with those under previous or competing FTAs; and

    (iv) making proof of origin and related administrative procedures predictable and business friendly.

The study analyzes RCEP's PSRO compared with those of the Comprehensive and Progressive Agreement for Trans-Pacific Partnership (CPTPP) and the ASEAN Trade in Goods Agreement (ATIGA). It does this using an innovative coding method based on manufacturing requirements, comparing more than 15,000 PSROs. The comparison shows that RCEP introduced several improvements over ATIGA and the CPTPP, yet does not simplify PSRO and related administrative requirements to their fullest extent. The analysis conducted in this study provides for a way forward and policy recommendations in these areas.

The results of the coding exercise analyzed in conjunction with tariffs and trade volumes suggest sectors where RCEP PSROs could be substantially reviewed toward greater convergence and simplification. More precisely, the results indicate areas where (a) PSROs could be made more lenient and (b) PSROs are converging across ATIGA, RCEP, and CPTPP.

This study recommends making use of the RCEP built-in agenda and of ongoing work conducted in other intergovernmental forums at the World Customs Organization, the World Trade Organization, and ASEAN to simplify rules of origin and related procedures. The analysis carried out in this study can serve as a basis for the elaboration of an ambitious policy agenda of PSRO convergence leading to a substantial simplification of rules of origin across Asia and the Pacific.

While the study's coding exercise should be expanded to cover PSROs in other ASEAN+1 and major bilateral FTAs, it already offers policy makers a unique way to reflect upon the effectiveness and efficiency of PSROs under RCEP's built-in agenda. The review should examine and expand convergence further, using the analysis and creating a road map based on the results of this study.

Further research on rules of origin, especially on their administration (e.g., proof of origin) in RCEP, ATIGA, and CPTPP—and progressively in other major FTAs—is critical. The administration of rules of origin is one of the most frequently reported nontariff measures representing a significant cost for firms. The ultimate policy objective is to leverage on areas of convergence identified in this study to foster simplification of rules of origin and reduce trade costs in Asia and the Pacific.

Introduction

Rules of origin are a core component of any trade deal and have been routinely quoted as among the most significant trade liberalizing accomplishments of the nascent Regional Comprehensive Economic Partnership (RCEP). With that said, the trading advantages of RCEP could be amplified if the current complexity of rules of origin used across overlapping free trade agreements in Asia and the Pacific were to be untangled. RCEP and its gradual approach to implementation may provide opportunity to simplify rules of origin, which will benefit manufacturers and exporters across the region. As a regional free trade agreement among 15 economies of the Asia and Pacific region (Figure 1) that entered into force on 1 January 2022,[1] the partnership is expected to provide a common platform for firms that had to juggle different sets of trading rules.

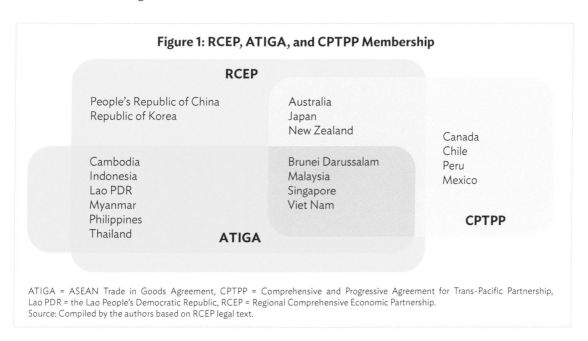

Figure 1: RCEP, ATIGA, and CPTPP Membership

ATIGA = ASEAN Trade in Goods Agreement, CPTPP = Comprehensive and Progressive Agreement for Trans-Pacific Partnership, Lao PDR = the Lao People's Democratic Republic, RCEP = Regional Comprehensive Economic Partnership.
Source: Compiled by the authors based on RCEP legal text.

RCEP has a distinct advantage over other free trade agreements (FTAs) since its wide geographic coverage makes its cumulation facilities[2] an important instrument for achieving efficiencies in production and trade. Yet, other factors are crucial to determining whether potential advantages can be turned into concrete opportunities for firms to turn to RCEP, and so give the partnership primacy over the existing tangle of FTAs in use.

---

[1]   The agreement entered into force on 1 January 2022, among the initial 10 signatory states that have deposited their instrument of ratification, acceptance or approval; Australia, Brunei Darussalam, Cambodia, the People's Republic of China, Japan, the Lao People's Democratic Republic, New Zealand, Singapore, Thailand, and Viet Nam. See https://www.meti.go.jp/english/press/2021/1103_001.html. In the Republic of Korea, the RCEP agreement entered into force on 1 February 2022. See https://www.meti.go.jp/english/press/2021/1206_002.html

[2]   Cumulation allows the treatment of products and inputs originating in RCEP parties to be considered as originating for the purpose of complying with the origin criterion of the goods regionally exported under the RCEP. See further details in Crivelli and Inama (2022) and Kang et. al (2020).

The first factor is the preferential margin[3] a firm may have in using RCEP instead of existing FTAs and their associated rules of origin. The margin depends on the tariffs offered under RCEP, the complexity of their structure, and rules for tariff differentials[4] affecting cumulation.

The second important factor is the extent and scope of cumulation, given that at entry into force the applicable RCEP provision on cumulation is limited to cumulation of originating materials (Crivelli and Inama 2021). Of note, the cumulation of working or processing within RCEP is going to be discussed during future review of the implementation stage of the RCEP built-in agenda.[5]

Third, proof of origin and its related administrative aspects comprise a crucial factor likely to determine whether firms will use RCEP over and above existing FTAs.

Adoption of an administrative system based on certifying authorities and certificate of origin rather than self-certification highlights that RCEP is taking a conservative stance that, for the time being, does not represent a significant departure from how existing FTAs approach administrative aspects of rules of origin (RoO). Only at a later stage and subject to the unfolding of the RCEP built-in agenda[6] can further openings and innovation be expected. The drafting complexity of the RCEP's Article 3.16 on proof of origin with different practices and timetables adopted by partners is revealing of the various schools of thought in this area.

Once these factors are considered, the role of product-specific rules of origin (PSRO) in determining the effective market access granted under RCEP becomes central to the debate about the value of its incremental market access over existing FTAs and their PSRO.

The purpose of this study is to provide an initial assessment of PSRO in RCEP. The analysis focuses on the leniency or stringency of PSRO in terms of manufacturing requirements, whenever possible. Comparison of the PSRO of RCEP with two other FTAs—the ASEAN Trade in Goods Agreement (ATIGA) and the Comprehensive and Progressive Agreement for Trans-Pacific Partnership (CPTPP)— is carried out. Given the overlapping membership (Figure 1), their PSRO can be considered as benchmarks for evaluating PSRO in RCEP.

---

[3]   The RCEP preferential margin is defined as the difference between the most-favored nation (nonpreferential) tariff rate and the reduced rate granted under RCEP.

[4]   See for a discussion of tariff differentials, Crivelli and Inama (2022) .

[5]   See para. 2 of Article 3.4 of the RCEP rules of origin: "2. The Parties shall commence a review of this Article on the date of entry into force of this Agreement for all signatory States. This review will consider the extension of the application of cumulation in paragraph 1 to all production undertaken and value added to a good within the Parties. The Parties shall conclude the review within five years of the date of its commencement, unless the Parties agree otherwise."

[6]   See para. 4 of Article 3.16 of chapter 3 of RCEP: "The Parties shall commence a review of this Article on the date of entry into force of this Agreement for all signatory States. This review will consider the introduction of Declaration of Origin by an importer as a Proof of Origin. The Parties shall conclude the review within five years of the date of its commencement, unless the Parties agree otherwise."

I.   Main Features of RCEP Rules of Origin

The RCEP RoO are the result of an evolution and gradual experiences gained in drafting RoO in earlier FTAs. In particular, the specific text on RoO contains a series of similarities with ATIGA and features that show the influence of different ways that Japan, Australia, and New Zealand have drafted RoO in their respective FTAs, reflecting their vast experience in the area.

The various iterations of ASEAN RoO included in ATIGA are well known. RCEP itself reflects the desire of ASEAN countries to imprint the ASEAN model of RoO in the wider regional agreement. Even so, RCEP includes several features unmatched in ATIGA.

One of the main differences is the pragmatic approach inherited from the CPTPP for a complete PSRO annex instead of making general RoO applicable across the board. Comparison of texts in Table 1 shows that RCEP has adopted the CPTPP text almost verbatim. This represents a significant improvement over ATIGA. To this end, RCEP resolves the lack of clarity in ATIGA about the sequencing of applications between general rules and PSRO.

RCEP adopts the concept of regional value content (RVC) which is common practice in Asian FTAs. It is important to note that the RVC concept embeds the notion of cumulation. In fact, given that the ad valorem percentage threshold is met as a region and not as individual country, this is a trade-friendly and trade-facilitating approach. However, one hiccup in RVC is that FTA members, especially in megaregional groups like RCEP and CPTPP, may adopt different tariff offers in their schedules toward partners. This means that additional provisions should be inserted in the FTA text (in this case, for RCEP) during implementation of the tariff phase-down, to allocate origin to one partner when two or more countries have been involved in the production of a good. Given the tariff differentials contained in RCEP and the lengthy transition periods of some tariff schedules, the RVC criterion for PSRO may be difficult to apply when the finished product is the result of production in two or more countries.

As shown in Table 2, the RCEP RVC calculation follows the CPTPP model in the definition of the build-down formula of RVC. However, similarities stop there since the RCEP build-up methodology is a carbon copy of the old ASEAN direct method.

In reality, the so-called direct and/or build-up formula in RCEP is not based on the value of originating materials, as it is in CPTPP and many other FTAs in Asia. Instead, it is a value-added calculation based directly on ATIGA. As such, it carries the shortcomings of a value-added methodology in calculating the ad valorem percentage.[7]

---

[7]   See Inama and Crivelli (2019), Section 3.1 on the Advantages and Disadvantages of Different Methodologies for Calculating the Ad Valorem Percentage Criterion.

Table 1: Comparison of Definition of Originating Products

RCEP	ATIGA	CPTPP

Article 3.2: Originating Goods
For the purposes of this Agreement, a good shall be treated as an originating good if it is:
(a) wholly obtained or produced in a Party as provided in Article 3.3 (Goods Wholly Obtained or Produced);
(b) produced in a Party exclusively from originating materials from one or more of the Parties; or
(c) produced in a Party using non-originating materials, provided the good satisfies the applicable requirements set out in Annex 3A (Product-Specific Rules), and meets all other applicable requirements of this Chapter.
	Article 28: Not Wholly Obtained or Produced Goods
	1. (a) For the purposes of Article 26(b), goods shall be deemed to be originating in the Member State where working or processing of the goods has taken place:
	    (i) if the goods have a regional value content (hereinafter referred to as "ASEAN Value Content" or the "Regional Value Content (RVC)") of not less than forty percent (40%) calculated using the formula set out in Article 29; or
	    (ii) if all non-originating materials used in the production of the goods have undergone a change in tariff classification (hereinafter 31 Chapter referred to as "CTC") at four-digit level (i.e. a change in tariff heading) of the Harmonized System.
	(b) Each Member State shall permit the exporter of the good to decide whether to use paragraph 1(a)(i) or 1(a)(ii) of this Article when determining whether the goods qualify as originating goods of the Member State.
	2. (a) Notwithstanding paragraph 1 of this Article, goods listed in Annex 3 shall qualify as originating goods if the goods satisfy the product-specific rules set out therein.
		Article 3.2: Originating Goods
		1. Except as otherwise provided in this Chapter, each Party shall provide that a good is originating where:
		    (a) the good is wholly obtained or produced entirely in the territory of one or both Parties, according to Article 3.4 (Wholly Obtained or Produced Goods);
		    (b) the good is produced entirely in the territory of one or both Parties, exclusively from materials whose origin complies with the provisions of this Chapter; or
		    (c) the good is produced in the territory of one or both Parties, using non-originating materials that conform to a change in tariff classification, a qualifying value content, or any other requirements, according to Article 3.5 (Not Wholly Obtained or Produced Goods).
		2. In addition to paragraph 1, the good shall meet the other applicable requirements under this Chapter.

ASEAN = Association of Southeast Asian Nations, ATIGA = ASEAN Trade in Goods Agreement, CPTPP = Comprehensive and Progressive Agreement for Trans-Pacific Partnership, RCEP = Regional Comprehensive Economic Partnership.
Sources: Compiled by authors from ATIGA, CPTPP, and RCEP official legal texts.

A positive point in the RVC calculation method used in RCEP is that in contrast to ATIGA, the cost of freight and insurance is deducted from the value of non-originating materials, which is in line with CPTPP. The deduction of cost of freight and insurance has progressively emerged as best practice in modern FTAs and is especially important for landlocked countries and for countries that are not part of, or are far from, logistics hubs. Transport costs make inputs more costly for such countries and they may be unduly penalized.

Such provision is inserted in para. 5 of Article 3.5 of RCEP:

"5. The following expenses may be deducted from the value of non-originating materials or materials of undetermined origin: (a) the costs of freight, insurance, packing, and other transport-related costs incurred in transporting the goods to the producer; (b) duties, taxes, and customs brokerage fees, other than duties that are waived, refunded, or otherwise recovered; and (c) costs of waste and spillage, less the value of any renewable scrap or by-products. Where the expenses listed in subparagraphs (a) through (c) are unknown or evidence is not available, then no deduction is allowed for those expenses."

Table 2: Comparison of RVC Calculations

RCEP	**Article 3.5: Calculation of Regional Value**
	Content 1. The regional value content of a good, specified in Annex 3A (Product-Specific Rules), shall be calculated by using either of the following formulas.
	(a) Indirect or Build-Down Formula $$RVC = \frac{FOB-VNM}{FOB} \times 100$$
	(b) Direct or Build-Up Formula $$RVC = \frac{VOM + Direct\ Labor\ Cost + Direct\ Overhead\ Cost + Profit + Other\ Cost}{FOB} \times 100$$
ATIGA	**Article 29: Calculation of Regional Value**
	Content 1. For the purposes of Article 28, the formula for calculating ASEAN Value Content or RVC is as follows:
	(a) Direct Method $$RVC = \frac{ASEAN\ Material\ Cost + Direct\ Labour\ Cost + Direct\ Overhead\ Cost + Other\ Cost + Profit}{FOB\ Price} \times 100$$
	(b) Indirect Method $$RVC = \frac{FOB\ Price - Value\ of\ Non\ Originating\ Materials, Parts\ or\ Goods}{FOB\ Price} \times 100$$
CPTPP	**Article 3.5: Regional Value Content**
	Content 1. Each Party shall provide that a regional value content requirement specified in this Chapter, including related Annexes, to determine whether a good is originating, is calculated as follows:
	(a) Focused Value Method: Based on the Value of Specified Non- Originating Materials $$RVC = \frac{Value\ of\ the\ Good - FVNM}{Value\ of\ the\ Good} \times 100$$
	(b) Build-down Method: Based on the Value of Non-Originating Materials $$RVC = \frac{Value\ of\ the\ Good - VNM}{Value\ of\ the\ Good} \times 100$$
	(c) Build-up Method: Based on the Value of Originating Materials $$RVC = \frac{VOM}{Value\ of\ the\ Good} \times 100$$
	(d) Net Cost Method (for Automotive Goods Only) $$RVC = \frac{NC - VNM}{NC} \times 100$$

ASEAN = Association of Southeast Asian Nations, ATIGA = ASEAN Trade in Goods Agreement, CPTPP = Comprehensive and Progressive Agreement for Trans-Pacific Partnership, FOB = freight on board, FVNM = Focused value of non-originating materials, NC = net cost, RCEP = Regional Comprehensive Economic Partnership, RVC = regional value content, VNM = value of non-originating materials, VOM = Value of originating materials.
Sources: Compiled by authors from ATIGA (Article 29), CPTPP (Article 3.5), and RCEP (Article 3.5).

II. The Form of PSRO in RCEP, ATIGA, and CPTPP

The form of PSRO is defined as the methodology used to draft PSRO.[8] The RCEP legal text contains a useful explanation of the various forms of PSRO in RCEP:

"(a) RVC40 means that the good must have a regional value content (hereinafter referred to as "RVC" in this Annex) of no less than 40 per cent as calculated under Article 3.5 (Calculation of Regional Value Content);

(b) CC [Change of Chapter] means that all non-originating materials used in the production of the good have undergone a Change of tariff classification (CTC) at the two-digit level of the Harmonized System;

(c) CTH [Change of Tariff Heading] means that all non-originating materials used in the production of the good have undergone a CTC at the four-digit level of the Harmonized System;

(d) CTSH [Change of Tariff Sub-Heading] means that all non-originating materials used in the production of the good have undergone a CTC at the six-digit level of the Harmonized System;

(e) WO [Wholly Obtained] means wholly obtained or produced in a Party as provided in Article 3.3 (Goods Wholly Obtained or Produced). For greater certainty, where the rule for a good is WO, the good can still meet the requirements to be treated as an originating good by being produced in a Party exclusively from originating materials from one or more of the Parties in accordance with subparagraph (b) of Article 3.2 (Originating Goods); and

(f) CR stands for chemical reaction rule. Any good that is a product of a chemical reaction shall be considered to be an originating good if the chemical reaction occurred in a Party. A "chemical reaction" is a process, including a biochemical process, which results in a molecule with a new structure by breaking intramolecular bonds and by forming new intramolecular bonds, or by altering the spatial arrangement of atoms in a molecule.

The following are not considered to be chemical reactions for the purposes of this definition:

(i) dissolving in water or other solvents;

(ii) the elimination of solvents including solvent water; or

(iii) the addition or elimination of water of crystallization."

RCEP adopts some of the ATIGA forms of drafting PSRO with a series of innovations and different drafting techniques. Innovations are most likely the result of negotiations with partners like Japan, Australia, and New Zealand that have used and elaborated different drafting forms for the PSRO inserted in their FTAs.

---

[8] For a discussion of the difference of "form" and "substance" of PSRO, see Hoekman and Inama (2018).

In general, increasing use is made of the Change of Tariff Classification (CTC) as a preferred PSRO drafting method. However, this has not gained universal acceptance since CTC is used in a variety of ways at different levels of disaggregation[9] and, as now discussed, is often combined with other forms of RoO (for instance, CTH or RVC in the case of ATIGA general rules).

Both RCEP and ATIGA use the CTC as a PSRO drafting form. In addition, and as shown in Table 3, for live animals of HS chapter 1, both RCEP and ATIGA require that the products are wholly obtained: i.e., that the live animals of chapter 1 are born and raised in RCEP or ATIGA countries respectively. With the application of a CTC, the drafting form of CPTPP for HS chapter 1 is completely different. First, the CPTPP breaks down PSRO at heading level, providing for a range of headings under which the PSRO apply and then requires a change of chapter (CC).

Table 3: Example of Different Uses of CTC and Drafting Techniques

HS Description	RCEP	ATIGA	CPTPP
Chapter 1 live animals	WO	WO	01.01 - 01.06 A change to a good of heading 01.01 through 01.06 from any other chapter.

ATIGA = ASEAN Trade in Goods Agreement, CPTPP = Comprehensive and Progressive Agreement for Trans-Pacific Partnership, CTC = change of tariff classification, HS = harmonized system, RCEP = Regional Comprehensive Economic Partnership, WO = wholly obtained.
Sources: Compiled by the authors based on RCEP, ATIGA, and CPTPP legal texts.

Since there is no antecedent in the HS to live animals[10] of chapter 1, the substantive requirement for a CC in the CPTPP is the same as in RCEP and ATIGA. In other words, to be considered as originating, the live animal of chapter 1 must be born and raised in a RCEP, ATIGA, or CPTPP partner country.

One of the first varieties of the use of the CTC methodology is the level of disaggregation in the HS.

Generally speaking, European Union FTAs use the HS mostly at the HS chapter and HS heading level while FTAs inspired by the Northern America model use the HS at CTH and CTSH level of disaggregation. Such variety is also applied in drafting an individual PSRO and in defining the number of PSRO. It is clear that a strict definition of PSRO at the CTSH level will produce a figure of about 5,244 PSRO, matching the number of tariff subheadings in the HS version currently applicable.

In practice, countries defining PSRO at CTSH level do not use such disaggregation for all HS chapters but tend to disaggregate more for sectors that are import-sensitive. For instance, the PSRO in the United States–Mexico–Canada Agreement (USMCA) clearly are not disaggregated at the HS subheading for chapter 16, Preparations of Meat, of Fish or of Crustaceans, Molluscs or Other Aquatic Invertebrates:[11]

---

[9]   The harmonized system is an international nomenclature for the classification of products based on the International Convention on the Harmonized Commodity Description and Coding System (HS convention) introduced on 1 January 1988. More than 200 economies and customs or economic unions are currently using the system as a basis for their national Customs tariffs (see World Customs Organization- http://www.wcoomd.org/en/topics/nomenclature/instrument-and-tools/hs_convention.aspx). The harmonized system is subdivided in chapters at 2-digits level, headings at 4-digits level, and subheading at 6-digits level. There is a variety of practices in drafting PSRO using CTC ranging from defining PSRO at chapter, heading, subheading level or a greater level of disaggregation. In addition, the form of the PSRO may also vary.

[10] In reality an antecedent is possible since embryos are classified in subheading 05.11.99. In any case, the animals would need to be born and have lived in the country where insemination had occurred: i.e., wholly obtained.

[11] USMCA Product-Specific Rules of Origin are found in Annex 4.B of the agreement.

"16.01-16.05 A change to heading 16.01 through 16.05 from any other chapter."

However, USMCA sets PSRO for peanut butter at subheading level:

"2008.11: A change to subheading 2008.11 from any other heading, except from heading 12.02."

The disaggregation even exceeds the HS subheading level (210320aa below is at tariff item level, 8 digits) going to what is referred to as tariff item level in USMCA in the case of tomato ketchup:

"2103.20.aa: A change to tariff item 2103.20.aa from any other chapter, except from subheading 2002.90."

The disaggregation level in defining PSRO is linked to the sensitivity of products: i.e., the more sensitive the product, the more disaggregated the definition may be at CTSH or a higher level of detail. This ensures that specific trade interests are safeguarded and, arguably, that PSRO are as clear and predictable as possible.

In RCEP, the PSRO are mostly but not always defined at the CTH or CTSH levels, as shown in Table 4. In fact, RCEP is unique in using PSRO at the chapter level, whereas ATIGA and CPTPP prefer more disaggregate levels in their PSRO definitions.

Table 4: Summary of PSRO
(Comparison of CPTPP, ATIGA, and RCEP)

FTA	Number of PSRO at Chapter Level	HS Chapters Covered	Number of PSRO at Heading Level	Number of PSRO at Subheading Level	Total PSRO
RCEP	33	1, 2, 6, 10, 14, 26, 33, 36, 37, 42, 45, 49, 57, 58, 59, 60, 61, 62, 65, 66, 67, 68, 69, 73, 82, 86, 88, 89, 92, 93, 94, 95, 97	732	1,311	2,076
ATIGA	0	N/A	0	2,735	2,735
CPTPP	0	N/A	892	2,067	2,959

ATIGA = ASEAN Trade in Goods Agreement, CPTPP = Comprehensive and Progressive Agreement for Trans-Pacific Partnership, FTA = free trade agreement, HS = harmonized system, PSRO = product-specific rules of origin, RCEP = Regional Comprehensive Economic Partnership.
Note: ATIGA legal text only shows PSRO listed at the 6-digit level.
Source: Compiled by the authors based on RCEP, ATIGA, and CPTPP legal texts on product-specific rules of origin.

RCEP includes 2,076 PSRO overall; 33 PSRO at the chapter level, 732 at the heading level, and 1,311 at the subheading level. Thus, about 63% of the total PSRO are at the subheading level. The CPTPP and ATIGA have none at the chapter level.

ATIGA only lists product-specific rules at the subheading (6-digit) level; general rules in the form of RVC or CTH apply to about 3,000 non-listed subheadings.[12]

CPTPP lists 892 PSRO in headings and 2,067 in subheadings, meaning almost 70% of the 2,959 total are at the subheading level.

---

[12]   See ATIGA Article 28 in Table 1 for the general rules and the link with PSRO.

Table 5 summarizes the forms of PSRO most used by RCEP, ATIGA, and CPTPP.

Table 5: Classification of PSRO
(Comparison of CPTPP, ATIGA, and RCEP)

	Number of PSRO using…										
	solely RVC	solely WO	solely CC	solely CTH	solely CC or CTH with CTH/ CTSH exceptions[a]	CC and RVC	CTH and RVC[b]	solely CTSH	CTSH and RVC	Specific working or processing	Multiple alternative requirements[c]
ATIGA											
HS Chapters	N/A	N/A	N/A	N/A	N/A	N/A	N/A	N/A	N/A	N/A	N/A
HS Headings	N/A	N/A	N/A	N/A	N/A	N/A	N/A	N/A	N/A	N/A	N/A
HS Subheadings	156	223	0	0	134	405	2,468	0	985	58	774
Total	**156**	**223**	**0**	**0**	**134**	**405**	**2,468**	**0**	**985**	**58**	**774**
RCEP											
HS Chapters	0	2	7	1	1	3	19	0	0	0	0
HS Headings	8	12	141	91	25	30	417	0	8	1	0
HS Subheadings	7	34	120	30	66	96	365	13	580	0	0
Total	**15**	**48**	**268**	**122**	**92**	**129**	**800**	**13**	**588**	**1**	**0**
CPTPP											
HS Chapters	0	0	0	0	0	0	0	0	0	0	0
HS Headings	5	0	202	431	100	21	64	0	0	18	41
HS Subheadings	7	0	139	169	131	74	338	1,041	89	66	23
Total	**12**	**0**	**341**	**600**	**231**	**95**	**402**	**1,041**	**89**	**84**	**64**

ATIGA = ASEAN Trade in Goods Agreement, CC = change of chapter, CPTPP = Comprehensive and Progressive Agreement for Trans-Pacific Partnership, CTH = change of tariff heading, CTSH = change of tariff subheading, FTA = free trade agreement, HS = harmonized system, PSRO = product-specific rules of origin, RCEP = Regional Comprehensive Economic Partnership, RVC = regional value content, WO = wholly obtained.

[a] Includes RVC in the case of ATIGA.
[b] In the case of ATIGA, this is the general rule, i.e., this rule applies for a HS heading unless otherwise stated.
[c] This is a column comprised of PSRO that have a narrative requiring specific working of processing; in many cases it is specific to the 6-digit code and thus all of these unique rules are compiled together for the purposes of this table.
Sources: Compiled by the authors based on RCEP, ATIGA, and CPTPP legal texts on product-specific rules of origin.

Table 5 contains in more detail the repartition of the PSRO and, in the case of ATIGA, the general rules (CTH or RVC40) expressed in number of PSRO subheadings.

It is clear that with 2,468 subheadings, the general ATIGA rule applies to the majority of subheadings. Yet, of most note is that RCEP and CPTPP apply the CTH or RVC 40 as PSRO in a significant number of chapters: as much as 19 chapters, 417 headings, and 365 subheadings in RCEP and 64 headings and 338 subheadings in the CPTPP. This points to a significant convergence among the three FTAs for a good number of PSRO.

Also of note is that the CPTPP uses the simple CTSH for as many as 1,041 subheadings. ATIGA and RCEP use similar PSRO in addition to an RVC in 985 subheadings in the case of ATIGA, and 580 subheadings for RCEP.

Potential scope for convergence exists in this area since the alternative RVC40 added to CTSH may be redundant in some HS chapters. A difference of form rather than substance can be observed on the use of the Wholly Obtained (WO) criteria as PSRO, which is used widely in ATIGA (223 subheadings) and RCEP (2 chapters,12 headings, and 34 subheadings) yet not used at all in CPTPP.

ATIGA stands out, with 774 PSRO using multiple alternative requirements. This peculiarity derives from the PSRO of ATIGA in the textile and clothing sector consisting of multiple alternatives: RVC, CTC, and specific working and processing rules. ATIGA also stands out for using 156 subheadings with an "RVC only" rule, while is seldom applied in RCEP and CPTPP.

Figures 2 to 4 combine the results of Table 5 with HS chapters where the different kinds of PSRO are used. These figures are particularly useful since they visually show the concentration of PSRO by HS chapters. More specifically, they depict the form of PSROs most used in each FTA and the concentration of these different forms of PSRO in various HS chapters.

The visual comparisons among Figures 2 to 4 reflect some characteristics of the three FTAs previously discussed. ATIGA (Figure 2) shows a concentration of the general rule (CTH or RVC40) along various HS chapters, especially so in HS chapter 29–30 (chemicals and medicaments), HS chapter 39 (plastics), and the industrial HS chapters 65–96.

The next highest concentration is chapters 84 and 85, where the CTSH/RVC criterion is widely used. As discussed, a high concentration of PSRO is also evident in the textile and clothing sector, in particular chapter 61 (garments knitted or crocheted), 62 (garments, not knitted or crocheted), and in chapters 52 (cotton) and 54 (man-made filaments), where the ATIGA PSRO is expressed as a mix of alternative requirements.

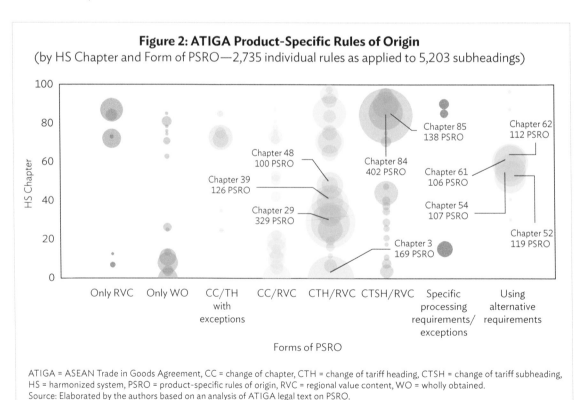

Figure 2: ATIGA Product-Specific Rules of Origin
(by HS Chapter and Form of PSRO—2,735 individual rules as applied to 5,203 subheadings)

ATIGA = ASEAN Trade in Goods Agreement, CC = change of chapter, CTH = change of tariff heading, CTSH = change of tariff subheading, HS = harmonized system, PSRO = product-specific rules of origin, RVC = regional value content, WO = wholly obtained.
Source: Elaborated by the authors based on an analysis of ATIGA legal text on PSRO.

Figure 3 shows in general a more diffusive spread of the different PSRO forms in RCEP than in ATIGA. The preponderance of the CTH or RVC form of PSRO is also apparent in RCEP even as it mainly covers certain chapters (HS chapter 29, chemicals) rather than being a pervasive feature, as in ATIGA. And like ATIGA, RCEP makes wide use of the CTSH/RVC form of PSRO, especially for chapters 84 and 85, and of the CC form—especially in the agriculture chapters, where both ATIGA and RCEP also use the wholly obtained form of PSRO.

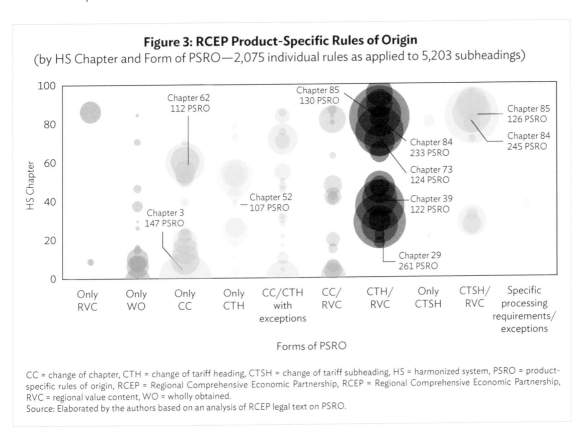

Figure 3: RCEP Product-Specific Rules of Origin
(by HS Chapter and Form of PSRO—2,075 individual rules as applied to 5,203 subheadings)

CC = change of chapter, CTH = change of tariff heading, CTSH = change of tariff subheading, HS = harmonized system, PSRO = product-specific rules of origin, RCEP = Regional Comprehensive Economic Partnership, RCEP = Regional Comprehensive Economic Partnership, RVC = regional value content, WO = wholly obtained.
Source: Elaborated by the authors based on an analysis of RCEP legal text on PSRO.

Conversely, the CC/RVC form of PSRO in RCEP is not featured in ATIGA, showing that RCEP has inherited some modern forms of drafting PSRO that are not present in ATIGA.

Figures 2 to 4 show the striking difference among ATIGA and RCEP on one hand and CPTPP on the other hand. Figure 4 depicts CPTPP's marked diffusion of PSRO forms used and spread widely among the HS chapters. Concentration is noted in chapter 29 and 84 as in other HS chapters of the use of the CTSH form of PSRO which is not matched in ATIGA and RCEP.

Simple CTH is also widely used by CPTPP in several HS chapters, especially chapter 84 (machinery). Alternative requirements in the form of specific working or processing are widely used by CPTPP for HS chapters 61 and 62 (garments) that are however very stringent when compared with RCEP and ATIGA, as is now discussed.

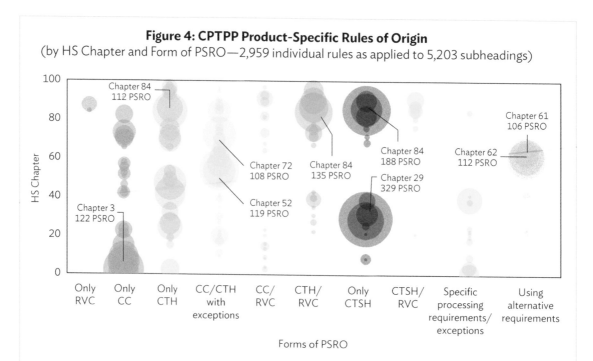

Figure 4: CPTPP Product-Specific Rules of Origin
(by HS Chapter and Form of PSRO—2,959 individual rules as applied to 5,203 subheadings)

CC = change of chapter, CPTPP = Comprehensive and Progressive Agreement for Trans-Pacific Partnership, CTH = change of tariff heading, CTSH = change of tariff subheading, HS = harmonized system, PSRO = product-specific rules of origin, RCEP = Regional Comprehensive Economic Partnership, RVC = regional value content, WO = wholly obtained.
Source: Elaborated by the authors based on an analysis of CPTPP legal text on PSRO.

III. Methodology to Assess PSRO Stringency or Leniency in RCEP

The stringency/leniency ratio of PSRO may be simply regarded as "what it takes" to meet the PSRO requirements. Some economic studies have codified the different forms of the CTC used in drafting to measure the stringency or leniency[13] of PSRO. However, such methodology does not account for the structure of the HS and its peculiarities. The HS was conceived as customs nomenclature and not for drafting PSRO, even as recently it has been used for this purpose.

A change of HS chapter requirement (CC) may be lenient or restrictive depending on the agriculture or industry sector where it is used. It could be extremely stringent in chapter 87 since cars and parts of cars are classified in the same chapter. Hence, even as the assembly of cars from different parts is a complex process, it would not generate the required CC. Conversely, grinding cereals of chapter 10 into flour (chapter 11) is a relatively simple process that would generate such CC. It follows that measuring and coding PSRO according to which CTC form is used does not reflect the reality of manufacturing. For example, as described in Crivelli and Inama (2021), a wholly obtained rule considered as extremely stringent for industrial goods is more lenient for exporters of live animals. While the form of the PSRO is the same in both cases, the codification of the stringency has to be different to reflect the economic reality of the respective sectors. The stringency of PSRO is varying across sectors and is not uniquely determined by the form in which PSRO is written. Codifying the stringency of RoO therefore requires careful examination of the meaning of the PSRO in terms of manufacturing requirements: it then becomes a question of what manufacturing is required to comply with the PSRO?

To address this complex issue, the most suitable approach is to adopt a methodology codifying PSRO based on the manufacturing requirements that are origin-conferring.

A recent study[14] followed this approach to assess the impact of the reform of EU GSP rules of origin of 2011. Table 6 provides examples of how RoO have been codified using manufacturing requirements. For apparel and clothing accessories under chapter 62 of the Harmonized System, the rule moved from a double to a single transformation requirement. It therefore became more lenient. Similarly, the PSRO for bicycles, classified under heading 8712 of the Harmonized System, has been codified as less stringent since the increase in the percentage of non-originating material, from 40% to 70%, made the rule easier to comply with.

In the case of olive oil classified under headings 1509 and 1510 of the Harmonized System, both the stringency and form of the rule have changed. From an initial change of tariff heading requirement, the rule became more stringent requiring that all vegetable materials (including olives) must be wholly obtained. The change in the drafting of the PSRO was also recorded in the codification. The fourth example shows a different scenario. While the new PSRO restricts the wholly obtained criterion to a specific range of products, the old and new rules present similar stringency since the fruits, nuts, or vegetables used to produce prepared or preserved tomatoes, mushrooms, and truffles classified under headings 2002 and 2003 of the Harmonized System are all included in chapters 7 or 8.[15]

---

[13] See for example Estevadeordal (2000), Estevadeordal, Harris, and Suominen (2009), and Harris (2007) on building an RoO restrictiveness index based on the form of PSRO.

[14] See Inama and Crivelli (2021).

[15] Some cases are not as clear cut and have been classified as undefined; their relative importance is marginal.

Table 6: Assessing PSRO Using Manufacturing Requirements
(Examples using the EU GSP reform of 2011)

Harmonized system level	Product-specific rules of origin		Change in stringency
	Former rule	New rule	
Chapter 62: Garments, not knitted or crocheted	Manufacturing from yarn	Manufacturing from fabric	Less stringent
Heading 8712: Bicycles	Manufacturing in which the value of non-originating material does not exceed 40% of the ex-works price of the finished products	Manufacturing in which the value of non-originating material does not exceed 70% of the ex-works price of the finished products	Less stringent
Headings 1509 and 1510: Olive oil and its fractions	Manufacturing from materials of any heading, except that of the product	Manufacturing in which all of the vegetable materials used are wholly obtained	More stringent and in different form
Headings 2002 and 2003: Tomatoes, mushrooms, and truffles prepared or preserved otherwise than by vinegar of acetic acid	Manufacturing in which all the fruits, nuts or vegetables used are wholly obtained	Manufacturing in which all the materials under chapters 7 and 8 used are wholly obtained	Similar

PSRO = product-specific rules of origin.
Source: Inama and Crivelli (2021)

This research deepens and expands the methodology and applies it to compare the PSRO of RCEP with those of CPTPP and ATIGA.

Another challenge to application of the methodology is the adoption of the CTC method in drafting PSRO in the three FTAs analyzed in this study. Simply put, it is necessary to make explicit the manufacturing requirements needed to generate the required CTC according to each PSRO. This task is extremely complicated and becomes even more difficult as products become more sophisticated; composed of different parts and made in different manufacturing or assembly operations.

Examples in the tables below elaborate on the adopted methodology.

Table 7 shows different PSRO for HS chapter 2, which classifies different kinds of meat and cuts of meat products. The CC requirement under ATIGA means that live animals of chapter 1 can be slaughtered to obtain meat in chapter 2, while the exclusion of chapter 1 in the PSRO of RCEP means that is not possible. This makes RCEP PSRO more restrictive than ATIGA and CPTPP. In addition, ATIGA adds the possibility of compliance by meeting the RVC 40 requirements, which could be achieved by cutting animal carcasses into smaller pieces, or deboning and using other cutting methods to reduce size.

Table 7: Meat Products

HS and products description	RCEP	ATIGA	CPTPP	Change in stringency
HS 0201 to HS 0210, Meat	CC except from Chapter 01	RVC40 or CC	A change to a good of heading 02.01 through 02.10 from any other chapter	RCEP PSRO is more stringent than CPTPP and ATIGA. ATIGA appears the more lenient.

ATIGA = ASEAN Trade in Goods Agreement, CC = change of chapter, CPTPP = Comprehensive and Progressive Agreement for Trans-Pacific Partnership, HS = harmonized system, PSRO = product-specific rules of origin, RCEP = Regional Comprehensive Economic Partnership, RVC = regional value content.
Sources: Compiled by the authors based on analysis of the RCEP, ATIGA, and CPTPP legal texts.

Table 8 depicts some PSRO for flours of chapter 11 that are obtained mostly by milling cereals classified in chapter 10 of the HS. The PSRO for subheading 110220 maize flour are similar for CPTPP and ATIGA and allow the non-originating cereals of chapter 10 to be used to make the flours of chapter 11 i.e., the grinding process is considered as origin-conferring. While drafted in a different manner, the CPTPP PSRO is substantially identical to a CC allowing the use of materials of chapter 10, i.e., cereals. The PSRO of RCEP, by contrast, is more stringent since it contains a CC with an explicit exclusion of materials classified in chapter 10.

However, the PSRO for CPTPP in subheading 110290—which classifies flours not made from wheat, meslin, and maize—contains an HS heading exception for heading 10.06 (rice). This means that non-originating rice cannot be used to make the flours of subheading 110290. In the specific case of rice flours RCEP has an equivalent stringency with CPTPP in excluding the use of non-originating rice. Yet ATIGA does not provide for the exclusion of non-originating rice, resulting in a more lenient PSRO.

Table 8: Flours

HS and products description	RCEP	ATIGA	CPTPP	Change in stringency
HS 110220 maize flour	CC except from Chapter 10	CC or RVC40	A change to a good of subheading 1102.20 from any other chapter	Same PSRO stringency for ATIGA and CPTPP, even more lenient for ATIGA since RVC option added.
HS 110290, cereal flours other than wheat, meslin maize	CC except from Chapter 10	CC or RVC40	A change to a good of subheading 1102.90 from any other chapter, except from heading 10.06	The exclusion in CPTPP of HS heading 10.06 means that the use of non-originating rice is not allowed. ATIGA PSRO is more lenient.

ATIGA = ASEAN Trade in Goods Agreement, CC = change of chapter, CPTPP = Comprehensive and Progressive Agreement for Trans-Pacific Partnership, HS = harmonized system, PSRO = product-specific rules of origin, RCEP = Regional Comprehensive Economic Partnership, RVC = regional value content.
Source(s): Compiled by the authors based on analysis of the RCEP, ATIGA, and CPTPP legal texts.

Table 9 compares the PSRO for heading 3920, which are similar across the three FTAs since they all allow a CTH that, in context of the specific heading 3920, means that blowing or extruding plates from polymers classified in other headings of chapter 39 is origin-conferring across the three FTAs. In addition, CPTPP provides a lower percentage (30%) under the build-up criteria, making the CPTPP slightly more lenient that PSRO under RCEP and ATIGA.

The PSRO for subheadings 392111 to 392190 provides for a CTSH in the case of CPTPP while PSRO for ATIGA and RCEP remain unchanged. In the context of heading 3921, the CTSH means not only that extruding and blowing from other headings of chapter 39 are origin- conferring but that other manufacturing processes such as coloring, printing, or vacuum deposition of metal are too. As a result, the CPTPP CTSH PSRO is more liberal than the RCEP and ATIGA.

Table 9: Article of Plastics

HS and products description	RCEP	ATIGA	CPTPP	Change in stringency
HS 3920 Other plates, sheets, film, foil and strip, of plastics, non-cellular and not reinforced, laminated, supported or similarly combined with other materials	RVC40 or CTH	RVC40 or CTH	A change to a good of heading 39.19 through 39.20 from any other heading; or No change in tariff classification required for a good of heading 39.19 through 39.20, provided there is a regional value content of not less than: (a) 30% under the build-up method; or (b) 40% under the build-down method.	CPPTP slightly more lenient than ATIGA and RCEP
3921 Other plates, sheets, film, foil and strip, of plastics	CTH or RVC 40	CTH or RVC40	A change to a good of subheading 3921.11 through 3921.90 from any other subheading	CPTPP more liberal as it allows CTSH

ATIGA = ASEAN Trade in Goods Agreement, CC = change of chapter, CPTPP = Comprehensive and Progressive Agreement for Trans-Pacific Partnership, CTH = change of tariff heading, CTSH = change of tariff subheading, HS = harmonized system, PSRO =product-specific rules of origin, RCEP = Regional Comprehensive Economic Partnership, RVC = regional value content.
Sources: Compiled by the authors based on analysis of the RCEP, ATIGA, and CPTPP legal texts.

Table 10 compares PSRO for selected garments of chapter 62, where the PSRO of CPTPP stand out as an example of complexity and stringency. The drafting methodology for CPTPP is based on CTC and requires a triple transformation process of spinning, weaving, and making up. This means in practice that a CPTPP producer cannot use non-originating yarn or fabric to make a chapter 62 garment, whereas both RCEP and ATIGA allow this.

Table 10: Clothing of Chapter 62

HS and product description	RCEP	ATIGA	CPTPP	Change in stringency
62.01 to 6208.	CC	A regional value content of not less than 40%; or A change to subheading 6201.11 from any other chapter and the good is both cut and sewn in the territory of any Member State; or Process Rules for Textile and Textile Products as set out in Attachment 1[a]	A change to a good of heading 62.01 through 62.08 from any other chapter, except from heading 51.06 through 51.13, 52.04 through 52.12, or 54.01 through 54.02; subheading 5403.33 through 5403.39, or 5403.42 through 5403.49; or heading 54.04 through 54.08, 55.08 through 55.16, 58.01 through 58.02, or 60.01 through 60.06, provided the good is cut or knit to shape, or both, and sewn or otherwise assembled in the territory of one or more of the Parties.	RCEP and ATIGA PSRO are more lenient than CPTPP

ATIGA = ASEAN Trade in Goods Agreement, CC = change of chapter, CPTPP = Comprehensive and Progressive Agreement for Trans-Pacific Partnership, HS = harmonized system, PSRO = product-specific rules of origin, RCEP = Regional Comprehensive Economic Partnership.
[a] Attachment 1 of ATIGA refers to some specific working or processing requirements that could be carried out on non-originating materials to get originating status. Such product-specific working or processing requirements are lenient insofar they often require a single processing stage, i.e., spinning of yarn, weaving of yarn into fabric, cut, make and trim for finished garments rather than the multiple processing requirements under the CPTPP.
Sources: Compiled by the authors based on analysis of the RCEP, ATIGA, and CPTPP legal texts.

Table 11 compares the PSRO for shoes of chapter 64. It is important to note that parts of shoes are classified in heading 6406. Therefore, a simple CTH—as provided under RCEP and ATIGA—means that the assembly of parts of shoes into finished shoes is origin-conferring. The PSRO under the CPTPP is much more stringent since it does not permit use of non-originating materials of heading 6406 except under strict conditions and a RVC requirement.

Table 11: Footwear

HS and product description	RCEP	ATIGA	CPTPP	Change in stringency
64.02. Sports footwear	RVC40 or CTH	RVC40 or CTH	A change to a good of heading 64.01 from any other chapter; or A change to a good of heading 64.01 from any other heading, except from heading 64.02 through 64.05, subheading 6406.10 or assemblies of uppers other than of wood of subheading 6406.90 provided there is a regional value content of not less than: (a) 45% under the build-up method; or (b) 55% under the build-down method.	RCEP and ATIGA PSRO are more lenient than CPTPP

ATIGA = ASEAN Trade in Goods Agreement, CPTPP = Comprehensive and Progressive Agreement for Trans-Pacific Partnership, CTH = change of tariff heading, HS = harmonized system, PSRO = product-specific rules of origin, RCEP = Regional Comprehensive Economic Partnership, RVC = regional value content.
Sources: Compiled by the authors based on analysis the of RCEP, ATIGA, and CPTPP legal texts.

Table 12 compares PSRO for monitors and screens, which are similar across the three FTAs and based on a CTH and an RVC. The only difference concerns the CPTPP, which provides an additional methodology for RVC calculation and a slightly lower percentage requirement under the build-up methodology. As a result, the level of stringency is similar with a slight positive bias toward CPTPP.

Under subheading 852842, ATIGA introduces a further alternative, with a lower RVC of 35% combined with a CTSH requirement. Given that components and parts necessary to assemble monitors are classified in other headings, one may wonder whether use of the alternative is practicable.

Table 12: Monitors

HS and product description	RCEP	ATIGA	CPTPP	Change in stringency
8528 Monitors and projectors, not incorporating television reception apparatus; reception apparatus for television, whether or not incorporating radio-broadcast receivers or sound or video recording or reproducing apparatus	RVC40 or CTH	RVC40 or CTH	A change to a good of heading 85.28 from any other heading; or No change in tariff classification required for a good of heading 85.28, provided there is a regional value content of not less than: (a) 30% under the build-up method; or (b) 40% under the build-down method; or (c) 50% under the focused value method taking into account only the non-originating materials of heading 85.28.	Same stringency
852842- Monitors; cathode-ray tube, capable of directly connecting to and designed for use with an automatic data processing machine of heading 8471	RVC40 or CTH	RVC40 or CTH or RVC35+CTSH	As above	Same stringency

ATIGA = ASEAN Trade in Goods Agreement, CPTPP = Comprehensive and Progressive Agreement for Trans-Pacific Partnership, CTH = change of tariff heading, CTSH = change of tariff subheading, HS = harmonized system, PSRO = product-specific rules of origin, RCEP = Regional Comprehensive Economic Partnership, RVC = regional value content.
Source: Compiled by the authors based on analysis of the RCEP, ATIGA, and CPTPP legal texts.

IV. Codifying PSRO Stringency and Leniency in RCEP

To perform the comparative analysis of PSRO in ATIGA, RCEP, and CPTPP, all PSRO have been compiled in a consolidated excel file disaggregated at the HS six digits level (2012 version). A line-by-line comparison and codification of about 15,000 observations has been carried out using a methodology based on the manufacturing requirement embedded in the form of the PSRO, as discussed in section 3. In this methodology, RCEP PSRO are used as a benchmark and the stringency or leniency of PSRO of CPTPP and ATIGA is measured against RCEP PSRO.

Two kinds of coding are elaborated. First, the detailed coding in Table 13 takes RCEP as the benchmark and the ATIGA and CPTPP PSRO are coded in terms of stringency against the RCEP PSRO. As RCEP is the benchmark, the detailed coding provides more information relating the PSRO in RCEP with those of ATIGA and CPTPP. Second, the simple coding (see Table 15) ranks the most lenient or stringent PSRO among the three FTAs. In short, using the simple coding scheme instead of detailed coding essentially forces a comparison between CPTPP and ATIGA through transitivity.

In the detailed coding, for instance, it is possible to have CPTPP less stringent than RCEP (3f), RCEP more stringent than ATIGA and CPTPP (1a), and ATIGA less stringent than RCEP (2e), which does not entail a comparison between CPTPP and ATIGA. In the simple scheme with only 1, 2, and 3, it will always appear they are either equal in stringency or that one is necessarily more stringent.

Advanced Codification

As discussed in section 3, coding has been carried out according to the industrial requirement needed to obtain originating status. Assessing such a requirement is straightforward in a number of cases when using the CTC or a specific working of processing requirement. However, requirements based on an RVC content are more difficult to assess because it is difficult to quantify what an RVC of 40% calculated on the free-on-board price of the finished product means for the manufacturing requirements of each industry sector.[16] In each case, the value judgments expressed depend on a series of parameters and the industry concerned.

The following codes have been used for the three FTA examined in this study:

RCEP codes
1a means RCEP more stringent than ATIGA and CPTPP
1b means RCEP more stringent than ATIGA
1c means RCEP more stringent than CPTPP
1d means RCEP less stringent than ATIGA and CPTPP
1e means RCEP less stringent than ATIGA
1f means RCEP less stringent than CPTPP

---

[16] The level of percentage and the practical use of the RVC 40 is among the areas where research is needed at firm and sectoral levels to better assess the user-friendliness of the PSRO.

ATIGA codes

2a means ATIGA more stringent than RCEP and CPTPP
2b means ATIGA more stringent than RCEP
2c means ATIGA more stringent than CPTPP
2d means ATIGA less stringent than RCEP and CPTPP
2e means ATIGA less stringent than RCEP
2f means ATIGA less stringent than CPTPP

CPTPP codes

3a means CPTPP more stringent than ATIGA and RCEP
3b means CPTPP more stringent than ATIGA
3c means CPTPP more stringent than RCEP
3d means CPTPP less stringent than ATIGA and RCEP
3e means CPTPP less stringent than ATIGA
3f means CPTPP less stringent than RCEP

Table 13 summarizes the results of this coding of the PSRO. Accordingly, results show that ATIGA has 1,339 PSRO less stringent than CPTPP and RCEP, while RCEP has 209 less stringent than CPTPP and ATIGA, and CPTPP has 576 less stringent than RCEP and ATIGA. According to this parameter, the ATIGA PSRO generally appear more liberal than those in RCEP and CPTPP.

The RCEP results show PSRO less stringent than those of CPTPP, with 1,135 coded as 1f in Table 13.

On one hand, the PSRO of CPTPP appear most stringent, with 1,427 occurrences more stringent than both ATIGA and RCEP. On the other hand, 576 CPTPP PSRO are less stringent than in both ATIGA and RCEP.

Qualifications and caveats are necessary to properly interpret these results. The ATIGA general rule as CTH or RVC alternative has influenced the comparison since it is applied as a default PSRO in cases where the parties to ATIGA did not negotiate PSRO or decided to apply general rules. The application of a CTH or RVC criterion in ATIGA thorough the HS chapters, as shown in Figure 2, has skewed the result of the comparison toward the ATIGA PSRO having more leniency. One may wonder if widespread application of the general rule of ATIGA is the product of an informed decision by A TIGA parties or the result of a default application.

In contrast, RCEP and CPTPP do not have general rules of origin, meaning that negotiators may have carefully scrutinized each HS chapter, resulting in a more accurate and vetted assessment of the implications of a given PSRO.

Another important consideration is to factor in the agriculture and industry sector in which the PSRO is applied and the value of intraregional trade in each of these sectors. For example, a wide divide exists in textile and clothing sector stringency between CPTPP, where PSRO are extremely restrictive and complex, and the much more lenient PSRO of RCEP and ATIGA. The restrictiveness of the CPTPP PSRO in HS chapters 50 to 63 influenced the overall results shown in Table 13. Yet it must be realized that the intraregional trade of these chapters does not constitute a significant part of overall intraregional RCEP trade, as is discussed later in this paper.

Table 13: Results of the PSRO Coding
(Comparison of CPTPP, ATIGA, and RCEP)

Code	Number of Subheadings		
ATIGA			
2a more stringent than RCEP and CPTPP	321	x	x
2b more stringent than RCEP	276	x	x
2c more stringent than CPTPP	0	x	x
2d less stringent than RCEP and CPTPP	1,339	x	x
2e less stringent than RCEP	282	x	x
2f less stringent than CPTPP	48	x	x
RCEP			
1a more stringent than ATIGA and CPTPP	x	327	x
1b more stringent than ATIGA	x	18	x
1c more stringent than CPTPP	x	85	x
1d less stringent than ATIGA and CPTPP	x	209	x
1e less stringent than ATIGA	x	2	x
1f less stringent than CPTPP	x	1,135	x
CPTPP			
3a more stringent than ATIGA and RCEP	x	x	1,427
3b more stringent than ATIGA	x	x	0
3c more stringent than RCEP	x	x	194
3d less stringent than ATIGA and RCEP	x	x	576
3e less stringent than ATIGA	x	x	6
3f less stringent than RCEP	x	x	315
Total	**2,226**	**1,776**	**2,518**

ATIGA = ASEAN Trade in Goods Agreement, CPTPP = Comprehensive and Progressive Agreement for Trans-Pacific Partnership, FTA = free trade agreement, HS = harmonized system, RCEP = Regional Comprehensive Economic Partnership.
The results of the coding shown in this table do not take into account the subheadings where convergence has been identified as discussed in section 4.3 below.
Source: Compiled by the authors based on analysis of the RCEP, ATIGA, and CPTPP PSRO.

Table 14 shows the results of coding excluding HS chapters 50 to 63, where the CPTPP counts 571 subheadings more liberal than ATIGA and RCEP, and 301 subheadings more liberal than RCEP.

Table 14: Results of PSRO Coding with the Exclusion of HS Chapters 50–63
(Comparison of CPTPP, ATIGA, and RCEP)

Code	Number of Subheadings		
ATIGA specific			
2a more stringent than RCEP and CPTPP	317	x	x
2b more stringent than RCEP	276	x	x
2c more stringent than CPTPP	0	x	x
2d less stringent than RCEP and CPTPP	589	x	x
2e less stringent than RCEP	263	x	x
2f less stringent than CPTPP	48	x	x
RCEP specific			
1a more stringent than ATIGA and CPTPP	x	313	x
1b more stringent than ATIGA	x	18	x
1c more stringent than CPTPP	x	80	x
1d less stringent than ATIGA and CPTPP	x	209	x
1e less stringent than ATIGA	x	2	x
1f less stringent than CPTPP	x	441	x
CPTPP specific			
3a more stringent than ATIGA and RCEP	x	x	736
3b more stringent than ATIGA	x	x	0
3c more stringent than RCEP	x	x	191
3d less stringent than ATIGA and RCEP	x	x	571
3e CPTPP less stringent than ATIGA	x	x	6
3f CPTPP less stringent than RCEP	x	x	301
Total	**1,493**	**1,063**	**1,805**

ATIGA = ASEAN Trade in Goods Agreement, CPTPP = Comprehensive and Progressive Agreement for Trans-Pacific Partnership, FTA = free trade agreement, HS = harmonized system, RCEP = Regional Comprehensive Economic Partnership.
The results of the coding shown in this table do not account for subheadings where convergence has been identified.
Source: Compiled by the authors based on analysis of the RCEP, ATIGA, and CPTPP PSRO.

The importance of using a series of additional parameters for values of intraregional trade and preferential margins to better assess and interpret the coding results is discussed in section 5. Figure 5 adds a qualification to the results, where it is clear that intraregional trade in textile and garments is worth $104 billion and accounts for 5% of total intra-RCEP trade.

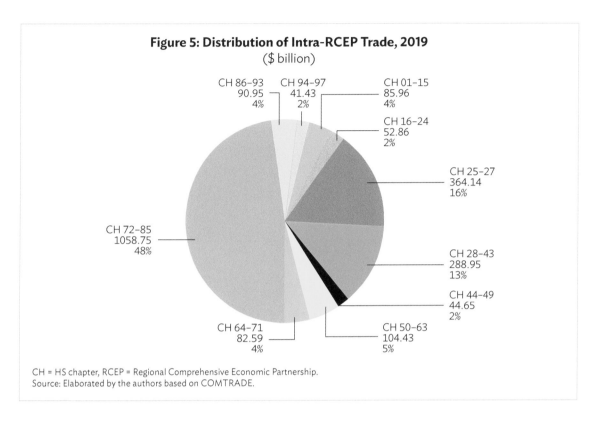

Figure 5: Distribution of Intra-RCEP Trade, 2019
($ billion)

CH 86–93
90.95
4%

CH 94–97
41.43
2%

CH 01–15
85.96
4%

CH 16–24
52.86
2%

CH 25–27
364.14
16%

CH 72–85
1058.75
48%

CH 28–43
288.95
13%

CH 44–49
44.65
2%

CH 64–71
82.59
4%

CH 50–63
104.43
5%

CH = HS chapter, RCEP = Regional Comprehensive Economic Partnership.
Source: Elaborated by the authors based on COMTRADE.

Simplified Coding Results

A simplified version of the coding is based on a scale of 1, 2, 3—where 1 is least restrictive, 2 is less restrictive, and 3 is most restrictive. FTAs have the same number for a given HS6 line where the rule is of the same stringency, so totals for 1, 2, and 3 will not equal the PSRO totals.

The results in Table 15 echo in simplified form the results of the more detailed coding. Among the three FTAs examined, ATIGA emerges with 3,321 PSRO least restrictive. The important point is that using such coding methodology, CPTPP records 2,706 PSRO of the least restrictive class, ranking better than RCEP, in which 1,774 PSRO are classed as least restrictive.

Table 15: Simple Coding

Code	Free Trade Agreement		
	ATIGA	**RCEP**	**CPTPP**
1	3,321	1,774	2,706
2	1,807	3,292	1,386
3	75	137	1,111

ATIGA = ASEAN Trade in Goods Agreement, CPTPP = Comprehensive and Progressive Agreement for Trans-Pacific Partnership, FTA = free trade agreement, RCEP = Regional Comprehensive Economic Partnership.
Source: Compiled by the authors based on analysis of the RCEP, ATIGA, and CPTPP PSRO.

RCEP appears to rank better under the second, less restrictive PSRO with 3,292 in this class while CPTPP has the most in the restrictive class (1,111), mostly deriving from the textile and garment sector.

As shown in Table 16, exclusion of the HS chapters 50–63 from the simple coding makes CPTPP appear less stringent with 2,687 subheadings, followed by ATIGA and RCEP. RCEP continues to have the most significant number of PSRO ranked as class 2, with 2,500 subheadings.

Table 16: Simple Coding Excluding HS Chapters 50–63

| Code | Free Trade Agreement | | |
	ATIGA	RCEP	CPTPP
1	2,534	1,770	2,687
2	1,806	2,500	1,301
3	67	137	419

ATIGA = ASEAN Trade in Goods Agreement, CPTPP = Comprehensive and Progressive Agreement for Trans-Pacific Partnership, FTA = free trade agreement, HS = harmonized system, RCEP = Regional Comprehensive Economic Partnership.
Source: Compiled by the authors based on analysis of the RCEP, ATIGA, and CPTPP PSRO.

Identifying Convergence

As was discussed in section 2, specific headings and at times entire HS chapters show almost identical PSRO for all the three FTAs. There are also conspicuous signs of convergence where two FTAs adopt similar or identical PSRO. As convergence can be a tremendous trade-facilitating tool to reduce the tangle of overlapping PSRO, a tailored analysis of convergence, based on the coding exercise, is presented in detail as follows.

- 1 means CPTPP and RCEP and ATIGA have identical or equivalent PSRO with or without different drafting

  Example:

HS subheading	CPTPP	RCEP	ATIGA
030111	CC	WO	WO

  ATIGA = ASEAN Trade in Goods Agreement, CC = change of chapter, CPTPP = Comprehensive and Progressive Agreement for Trans-Pacific Partnership, HS = harmonized system, RCEP = Regional Comprehensive Economic Partnership, WO = wholly obtained.

  In the example above RCEP and ATIGA have identical PSRO while CPTPP uses a change of chapter (CC). A change of chapter in this case means that the fish of heading 03011 has to be born and raised in CPTPP resulting to equivalent stringency with RCEP and ATIGA.

- 1x means RCEP and CPTPP have identical PSRO with ATIGA having an RVC or CTH rule (ATIGA general rule)

  Example:

HS subheading	CPTPP	RCEP	ATIGA
030211	CC	CC	CTH or RVC40

  ATIGA = ASEAN Trade in Goods Agreement, CC = change of chapter, CPTPP = Comprehensive and Progressive Agreement for Trans-Pacific Partnership, CTH = change of tariff heading, HS = harmonized system, RCEP = Regional Comprehensive Economic Partnership, RVC = regional value content.

- 1z means RCEP and ATIGA have identical or equal PSRO with CPTPP showing diverging PSRO. Example:

HS subheading	CPTPP	RCEP	ATIGA
200941	CC except from subheading 080430	CC or RVC 40	CC or RVC40

ATIGA = ASEAN Trade in Goods Agreement, CC = change of chapter, CPTPP = Comprehensive and Progressive Agreement for Trans-Pacific Partnership, HS = harmonized system, RCEP = Regional Comprehensive Economic Partnership, RVC = regional value content.

Under this example of subheading 200941 (pineapple juice) RCEP and ATIGA have identical PSRO while CPTPP excludes heading 080430 classifying fresh pineapple, the main ingredient to make pineapple juice, making the PSRO more restrictive.

The summary results, shown in Table 17, show significant signs of convergence given that as many as 769 subheadings have identical PSRO across the three FTAs and as many as 1,621 subheadings report RCEP and ATIGA with similar PSRO while the CPTPP PSRO diverge. There is also considerable convergence between RCEP and CPTPP, with ATIGA not matching mainly because the default general rule CTH or RVC 40 has been used.

Table 17: Convergence Count Summary

	Full convergence	RCEP and CPTPP are the same but ATIGA diverges	RCEP and ATIGA are the same but CPTPP diverges
Total number of HS subheadings	769	719	1,621

ATIGA = ASEAN Trade in Goods Agreement, CPTPP = Comprehensive and Progressive Agreement for Trans-Pacific Partnership, HS = harmonized system, RCEP = Regional Comprehensive Economic Partnership.
Source: Compiled by the authors based on analysis of the RCEP, ATIGA, and CPTPP PSRO.

Table 18 shows the total number of subheadings where PSRO are identical in terms of stringency even if a different drafting form is used.

Table 18: Full Convergence
(RCEP, CPTPP, and ATIGA are the same [RCEP 1, CPTPP 1, ATIGA 1])

Coding			
RCEP	CPTPP	ATIGA	Number of HS subheading
1	1	1	769
		Total	769

ATIGA = ASEAN Trade in Goods Agreement, CPTPP = Comprehensive and Progressive Agreement for Trans-Pacific Partnership, HS = harmonized system, RCEP = Regional Comprehensive Economic Partnership.
Source: Compiled by the authors based on analysis the of RCEP, ATIGA, and CPTPP PSRO.

The partial convergence number among ATIGA and RCEP reported in Table 17 counting a total of 1,621 headings shows, on one hand, the influence that ATIGA may have played during negotiations and on the other hand, the potential for greater convergence among the three FTAs. While such partial convergence exists between ATIGA and RCEP the divergence with CPTTP may take different forms according to the coding contained in Table 19. A notable remark can be made about the 457 subheadings where CPTPP results less stringent than ATIGA and RCEP. This finding shows that when ATIGA and RCEP are converging, CPTPP is less stringent in a significant number of subheadings. Further analysis should be carried out to identify the industrial sectors where such occurrence takes places and assess the underlying reasons.

Table 19: Partial Convergence I
(RCEP and ATIGA are the same [RCEP 1 and ATIGA 1] but CPTPP is divergent)

RCEP	CPTPP	ATIGA	Number of HS subheading
1	1z RCEP and ATIGA have equal stringency with CPTPP divergent PSRO	1	900
1	3a more stringent than ATIGA and RCEP	1	234
1	3d less stringent than RCEP and ATIGA	1	457
1	3f less stringent than ATIGA	1	30
		Total	1,621

ATIGA = ASEAN Trade in Goods Agreement, CPTPP = Comprehensive and Progressive Agreement for Trans-Pacific Partnership, HS = harmonized system, RCEP = Regional Comprehensive Economic Partnership.
Source: Compiled by the authors based on analysis of the RCEP, ATIGA, and CPTPP PSRO.

Table 20 shows the convergence among RCEP and CPTPP, totaling 719 subheadings. The divergence of ATIGA in 455 subheadings is mainly due to the default adoption of the ATIGA CTH/RVC 40 general rules that may be adjusted to create greater convergence. In fact, 197 subheadings are less stringent in ATIGA than in the converging RCEP and CPTPP PSRO. As in the case of the CPTPP divergence illustrated above there is a need to further detail the analysis to identify the specific industrial sectors and the possible underlying causes of such divergence.

Table 20: Partial Convergence II
(RCEP and CPTPP are the same [RCEP 1 and CPTPP 1] but ATIGA is divergent)

RCEP	CPTPP	ATIGA	Number of HS subheading
1	1	1x means RCEP and CPTPP have identical PSRO while ATIGA has an RVC or CTH rule	455
1	1	2a more stringent than RCEP and CPTPP	63
1	1	2d less stringent than RCEP and CPTPP	197
1	1	2f less stringent than CPTPP	4
		Total	719

ATIGA = ASEAN Trade in Goods Agreement, CPTPP = Comprehensive and Progressive Agreement for Trans-Pacific Partnership, HS = harmonized system, RCEP = Regional Comprehensive Economic Partnership.
Source: Compiled by the authors based on analysis of the RCEP, ATIGA, and CPTPP PSRO.

The results of this convergence exercise have significant value for policy recommendations as they signal to policy makers and negotiators routes for streamlining PSRO among the three FTAs.

V. Matching the Results of Coding with Trade and Tariff Data

The coding exercise offers potential to draw a series of informed policy recommendations about the built-in agenda of RCEP, especially in making the case for greater convergence among the three FTAs.

Table 21 matches the comparative matrix of PSRO built for this study with intraregional trade volumes by descending order, showing the first 10 HS subheadings. The scope of the exercise is to show the potential for greater PSRO convergence and to identify divergent PSRO with significant trade volume. This exercise is particularly important to inform the built-in agenda of RCEP. Total convergence is observed in the first two HS subheadings, where PSRO are identical. Some divergence is noted in case of minerals (iron ore and gold), where consultations may lead to further convergence. Some divergence may be noted in subheading 847130, where CPTPP and ATIGA appear to have the most liberal PSRO.

Table 21: RCEP Intra-Imports, 2019

(Top 10 HS subheadings sorted descending order according to intra-trade value, $millions)

HS code	Description	Value ($'000s)	No. of tariff items	MFN Rate			PSRO			Convergency	Principal Importers					
				Ave.	Min.	Max.	ATIGA	CPTPP	RCEP		Country code	Trade share (%)	Country code	Trade share (%)	Country code	Trade share (%)
(1)	(2)	(3)	(4)	(5)	(6)	(7)	(8)	(9)	(10)	(11)	(12)	(13)	(14)	(15)	(16)	(17)
854231	Electronic integrated circuits; processors and controllers, whether or not combined with memories	81,601	32	1.5	0	8.0	RVC40 or CTSH	CTSH or RVC	CTSH or RVC40	1	CHN	73.9	SGP	6.9	ROK	6.7
854232	Electronic integrated circuits; memories	78,163	33	1.5	0	8.0	RVC40 or CTSH	CTSH or RVC	CTSH or RVC40	1	CHN	70.5	ROK	16.9	SGP	5.0
260111	Iron ores and concentrates; non-agglomerated	72,980	24	0.9	0	5.0	RVC40 or CTH	CTH	CTH	1x	CHN	84.3	JPN	7.7	ROK	6.4
854239	Electronic integrated circuits; n.e.c. in heading no. 8542	71,802	27	1.5	0	8.0	RVC40 or CTSH	CTSH or RVC	CTSH or RVC40	1	CHN	31.5	SGP	26.8	VIE	21.3
851770	Telephone sets and other apparatus for the transmission or reception of voice, images or other data	46,275	135	2.5	0	15.0	RVC40 or CTH	CTH or RVC	CTH or RVC40	1	CHN	39.9	VIE	28.2	ROK	11.7
851712	Telephones for cellular networks or for other wireless networks	36,752	30	1.0	0	10.0	RVC40 or CTH or RVC35+ CTSH	CTSH	CTSH or RVC40	1z	JPN	42.0	SGP	13.2	AUS	10.7
847330	Machinery; parts and accessories (other than covers, carrying cases and the like) of the machines of heading 8471	24,809	33	1.2	0	8.0	RVC40 or CTH	CTH or RVC	CTH or RVC40	1	CHN	33.7	ROK	16.3	SGP	14.9

continued on next page

Table 21 continued

HS code	Description	Value ($'000s)	No. of tariff items	MFN Rate			PSRO			Convergency	Principal Importers					
				Ave.	Min.	Max.	ATIGA	CPTPP	RCEP		Country code	Trade share (%)	Country code	Trade share (%)	Country code	Trade share (%)
852990	Reception and transmission apparatus; for use with the apparatus of heading no. 8525 to 8528	20,746	164	4.1	0	15.0	RVC40 or CTH	CTH or RVC	CTH or RVC40	1	CHN	38.6	ROK	20.6	VIE	13.3
847130	Automatic data processing machines; portable, weighing not more than 10kg, consisting of at least a central process	20,643	27	1.0	0	7.0	RVC40 or CTSH	CTSH	CTH or RVC40	1z[a]	JPN	39.5	AUS	16.8	ROK	12.9
710812	Metals; gold, non-monetary, unwrought (but not powder)	19,998	17	0.7	0	5.0	RVC40 or CTH	CC	CC or RVC40	1z	CHN	64.0	THA	11.7	AUS	9.3

ATIGA = ASEAN Trade in Goods Agreement, AUS = Australia, CC = change of chapter, CHN = People's Republic of China, CPTPP = Comprehensive and Progressive Agreement for Trans-Pacific Partnership, CTH = change of tariff heading, CTSH = change of tariff subheading, HS = harmonized system, JPN = Japan, ROK = Republic of Korea, MFN = most favored nation, PSRO = product-specific rules of origin, RCEP = Regional Comprehensive Economic Partnership, RVC = regional value content, SGP = Singapore, THA = Thailand, VIE = Viet Nam.

[a] In this specific case the PSRO of ATIGA and RCEP appear to be formally different as they provide for a CTSH and CTH besides the possibility of meeting RVC. In reality these PSRO are equivalent because parts of HS subheadings 847130 are classified in heading 8473. Similarly, in the case of gold for the subheading 710812, the CTH or CC have equivalent manufacturing requirements.

Source: Compiled by the authors based on analysis of the RCEP, ATIGA, and CPTPP PSRO and UN COMTRADE data.

Table 22 shows the result of a similar exercise using the comparative table of PSRO built for this study matched with intraregional trade, with the highest MFN rates applicable sorted in descending order and the first 10 subheadings displayed. The table shows that the majority of products with high MFN rates are agricultural products with stringent PSRO. The volume of trade is significantly smaller than trade covered in Table 21, with only two subheadings more than $1 billion worth of trade: cassava (subheading 071410) and rice (subheading 100630). The PSRO already show a consistent degree of convergence that may be improved. Further analysis should be conducted on how other factors such as direct shipment provisions of third country invoicing may affect the utilization of trade preferences under RCEP for these products.

Table 22: MFN rates and RCEP Intra-Imports, 2019

(Top 10 HS subheadings sorted in descending order according to average MFN rate)

HS code	Description	Intra-trade value ($, 000s)	No. of tariff items	MFN Rate Ave.	MFN Rate Min.	MFN Rate Max.	PSRO ATIGA	PSRO CPTPP	PSRO RCEP	Convergency	Principal importers Country code	Principal importers Trade share (%)	Principal importers Country code	Principal importers Trade share (%)	Principal importers Country code	Principal importers Trade share (%)
(1)	(2)	(3)	(4)	(5)	(6)	(7)	(8)	(9)	(10)		(11)	(12)	(13)	(14)	(15)	(16)
100850	Cereals; quinoa (Chenopodium quinoa)	577	8	105.5	0	800.3	WO	CC	WO	1	NZL	51.5	SGP	26.7	PHI	9.1
100710	Cereals; grain sorghum, seed	1,507	9	99.1	0	779.4	WO	CC	WO	1	PHI	66.2	NZL	21.0	JPN	4.2
110820	Inulin	1,009	13	73.6	0	800.3	RVC40 or CC	CC	CC	1x	PHI	36.1	IDN	21.1	JPN	14.4
100610	Cereals; rice in the husk (paddy or rough)	45,706	23	72.0	0	513.0	WO	CC	WO	1	PHI	43.0	VIE	35.6	PRC	18.1
100890	Cereals; n.e.c. in chapter 10	3,529	14	70.6	0	800.3	WO	CC	WO	1	THA	48.1	PRC	21.0	IDN	14.6
071410	Vegetable roots and tubers; manioc (cassava),	1,135,116	46	68.9	0	887.4	WO	CC	CC	1	PRC	56.5	THA	22.0	VIE	17.1
100410	Cereals; oats, seeds	7,393	10	62.4	0	554.8	WO	CC	WO	1	MYS	70.8	JPN	27.8	SGP	0.5

continued on next page

Table 22 continued

HS code	Description	Intra-trade value ($ '000s)	No. of tariff items	MFN rate			PSRO			Convergency	Principal importers					
				Ave.	Min.	Max.	ATIGA	CPTPP	RCEP		Country code	Trade share (%)	Country code	Trade share (%)	Country code	Trade share (%)
151550	Vegetable oils; sesame oil and its fractions, whether or not refined, but not chemically modified	41,086	33	56.0	0	630.0	CC or RVC or no CTC provided good produced by refining	CC or RVC	CC	Partial convergence[a]	AUS	22.0	SGP	18.6	IDN	15.6
090210	Tea, green; (not fermented), in immediate packing of a content not exceeding 3kg	51,215	25	53.6	0	513.6	RVC40 or CC	CC or RVC	WO	Partial convergence	MYS	43.7	SGP	14.2	IDN	9.0
100630	Cereals; rice, semi-milled or wholly milled, whether or not polished or glazed	2,768,507	49	53.2	0	513.0	WO	CC	WO	1	PHI	36.1	PRC	30.5	MYS	13.1

ATIGA = ASEAN Trade in Goods Agreement, AUS = Australia, CC = change of chapter, PRC = People's Republic of China, CPTPP = Comprehensive and Progressive Agreement for Trans-Pacific Partnership, HS = harmonized system, IDN = Indonesia, JPN = Japan, MFN = most favored nation, MYS = Malaysia, NZL = New Zealand, PHI = the Philippines, PSRO = product-specific rules of origin, RCEP = Regional Comprehensive Economic Partnership, RVC = regional value content, SGP = Singapore, THA = Thailand, WO = Wholly Obtained, VIE = Viet Nam.

a   In this specific case as in the case of tea of heading 090210 (row below) partial convergence has been detected among ATIGA and CPTPP, while RCEP is divergent.

Source: Compiled by the authors based on analysis of the RCEP, ATIGA, and CPTPP PSRO and UN COMTRADE data.

VI. Conclusions and Recommendations

The results of the analysis in this study provide an agenda for the future of PSRO in RCEP and Asian FTAs, based on the following observations:

- Given that more than 30 FTAs have been signed in the RCEP region, including ASEAN plus one FTAs[17] and bilateral FTAs negotiated among RCEP parties, firms trading in the region must deal with hundreds of thousands applicable and competing PSRO. This makes the use of FTAs costly and complex. Comparison in this paper of more than 15,000 PSRO in three regional FTAs highlights that RCEP achieves a number of improvements over ATIGA and CPTPP. However, RCEP does not reach the pinnacle of PSRO simplification, even if it absorbs several positive lessons. Indeed, RCEP results show 1,135 PSRO are less stringent than CPTPP but these are concentrated in just one sector, textile and garments, which accounts for only 5% of trade between RCEP member states. Moreover, this sector will not be the main driver of these economies in the future.

- The results of the coding exercise analyzed in conjunction with tariffs and trade volumes offer the possibility of identifying PSRO that the built-in agenda of RCEP and other intergovernmental forums could review substantially as part of a wide effort to converge and simplify the PSRO.

- The results, both of comparative analysis and the coding exercise, highlight the conspicuous number of PSRO where the three FTAs converge to identical or similar rules. While the coding exercise should be enlarged to cover the other ASEAN plus one FTA PSRO and the main bilateral FTAs, it already offers a unique opportunity for policy makers to review the effectiveness and efficiency of PSRO under the RCEP built-in agenda. Such a review could further examine and expand convergence with the support of informed analysis and a road map drawn from this study's results. More specifically, a clear document should be elaborated to show policy makers

  (i) PSRO where convergence has been identified as a feasible target to achieve greater simplification,

  (ii) PSRO where partial convergence has been identified with options to get to full convergence, and

  (iii) PSRO where divergence has been detected with possible options to get to partial convergence or alternative solutions.

---

[17] ASEAN–PRC Free Trade Area (ACFTA), ASEAN–Japan Comprehensive Economic Partnership (AJCEP), and ASEAN–Korea Free Trade Area (AKFTA).

- The present PSRO study and its expansion should be accompanied by new research into rules of origin and in particular their administration (i.e., proof of origin) among RCEP, ATIGA, and CPTPP—and progressively to other major FTAs. This is an extremely important area that makes RoO one of the most reported nontariff measure and a cost burden for firms. In the area of RoO administration, no full-fledged studies have been undertaken to identify convergence on good practices and report the lessons learned to policy makers. Such research, accompanied by analysis of PSRO, will form a complete package of actionable reforms to address the complexities of RoO, proof of origin, and related administrative issues.

- Continued research in the areas outlined above is important. Research findings with appropriate policy advocacy will help policy makers and stakeholders move toward reforms for convergence and best practice. The ultimate aim is to simplify and converge rules of origin and their administration in FTAs across the whole of Asia and the Pacific. This is a regional public good worth pursuing.

References

Association of Southeast Asian Nations (ASEAN). 2009. ASEAN Trade in Goods Agreement (ATIGA). https://www.asean.org/wp-content/uploads/images/2013/economic/afta/atiga%20interactive%20rev4.pdf

Comprehensive and Progressive Agreement for Trans-Pacific Partnership (CPTPP). 2015. Legal texts. https://www.dfat.gov.au/trade/agreements/not-yet-in-force/tpp/Pages/tpp-text-and-associated-documents

Crivelli, P. and S. Inama. 2021. *Making RCEP Successful Through Business-friendly Rules of Origin.* Asian Development Blog. Manila. https://blogs.adb.org/blog/making-rcep-successful-through-business-friendly-rules-origin

Crivelli, P. and S. Inama. 2022. A Preliminary Assessment of the Regional Comprehensive Economic Partnership. *ADB Brief.* Manila: Asian Development Bank.

Estevadeordal, A. 2000. Negotiating Preferential Market Access: The Case of the North American Free Trade Agreement. *Journal of World Trade.* 34 (1). pp. 141–66. February.

Estevadeordal, A., J. Harris, and K. Suominen. 2009. Multilateralising Preferential Rules of Origin around the World. *IDB Working Paper Series.* No. IDB-WP-137.

Harris, J. 2007. Measurement and Determination of Rules of Origin in Preferential Trade Agreements. *PhD Dissertation.* College Park: University of Maryland.

Inama, S. and P. Crivelli. 2019. Convergence on the Calculation Methodology for Drafting Rules of Origin in FTAs Using the Ad Valorem Criterion. *Global Trade and Customs Journal.* 14 (4). pp. 146–53.

Inama, S. and P. Crivelli. 2021. Getting to Better Rules of Origin for LDC Using Utilization Rates. UNCTAD/ALDC/2019/3, eISBN: 978-92-1-005550-5. https://unctad.org/webflyer/getting-better-rules-origin-ldcs-using-utilization-rates

Hoekman, B. and S. Inama. 2018. Harmonization of Rules of Origin: An Agenda for Plurilateral Cooperation? *East Asian Economic Review.* 22 (1). pp. 3–28. March. doi: 10.11644/KIEP.EAER.2018.22.1.336

Kang, J.W., P. Crivelli, M.C. Tayag, and D. Ramizo. 2020. Regional Economic Partnership: Overview and Economic Impact. *ADB Brief.* No. 164. Manila: Asian Development Bank.

Regional Comprehensive Economic Partnership Agreement (RCEP). 2020. Legal texts. https://rcepsec.org/legal-text/

Lightning Source UK Ltd.
Milton Keynes UK
UKHW052335060622
404035UK00017B/412

9 789292 694838